I(DEAL)

From Overcoming to Becoming

Jahmad D. Canley

ISBN: 978-0-578-77195-3

Printed in the United States of America

i

Table of Contents

Foreward

I have known Jahmad Canley for over fifteen years. He is brilliant.

The very best at helping people achieve and explode beyond where they currently think their abilities and potential lie.

He believes everyone should do everything possible to secure for self, and those important to them, all that is possible rather than to become or remain dependent on others. You provide the clarity of your dreams and your desired end results. Jahmad provides you the why and the how, to create that pathway to your dreams and to those desired results you seek.

The award winning filmmaker Barry Levinson shared that when he is pitched a script or idea for a new movie, play or series, he asks the question, "What is the movies poster"? Why? He is asking can the movies premise be captured in a single image. If it can, it presents a future memory, an emotional connection that is compelling to the viewer who then will want to see the movie.

When you can create a clear image of what is important to you, that clear image will expand your awareness, your identity and your effectiveness and bring you to a higher level of being.

Jahmad's whole premise in his book is to provide that pathway.

To help us achieve what is ideal and essential to living a life of value and not get caught or trapped in living a life of second hand values or wants.

Jack Fitterer, CEO Emeritus. The Pacific Institute, Inc.

Dedication

This book is dedicated to all those who have helped me to realize and create my Ideal life.

To my parents, Jackie and Willie, and my sister Nikkiesha, who were my first teachers and taught me to believe in myself. You supported me and my dreams throughout my life. You always gave me the space to dream and to think in Ideals, even when you may not have agreed or understood. That foundation became my launching pad to fly. I love you. Thank you.

To my mentors, who have poured into me when they didn't have to. You allowed me to learn from you and provided great counsel over many years. You are too many to name, but please know that I appreciate you all. I cherish every morsel of wisdom you have shared with me in all aspects of my life.

To my children, who are the most important stories I will ever have a hand in writing. When I first had the idea to write a book, there were only two of you and now there are four. I love you more than words can ever express. You are my constant motivation to strive for my Ideal. I pray that, in addition to being your father, I am a model and mentor for you. I also want you to believe-- to know--that you have greatness in you; I see you use it in magnificent ways every day.

To my wife, Atiya, who always believes in me. Thank you for believing in me even at times when I didn't believe in myself. Thank you for loving me like only you can. Not only do you make me want to be my best self, you help me to be my best self. You are the true MVP of our family and always the hero in my story. You are my Ideal. I'm so thankful that I get to continue to fall in love with you every day.

To my brother Jamila Jones, you are the Ideal friend. I can't remember a time when I needed help and you didn't answer the call.

And to my family and friends who have encouraged me to write this book over the years, and to my clients and supporters for letting me share your stories, thank you!

Introduction

I was convinced I was going to lose, and worse, I was going to look foolish in front of everyone.

It was Wednesday and the election of our grade school president was in two days. Any confidence I had was slipping away. At best my posters were decent, and while I'd campaigned along with the other 10-year-old candidates, I was pretty sure I was the underdog.

As I sat at the dinner table, imagining the double dread of giving my speech and then losing in front of the entire student body gathered in the auditorium, my parents in their attempt to calm me down asked the question that was racing through my mind: *Why had I run for president in the first place?*

I cleared my throat, which is to say, I shook off the negative thoughts, and then listed the positive ways I thought I could change the school. Next, my parents asked me what I was afraid of and I shared my vision of blowing my speech and losing in front of everybody.

What my parents did next was key. Instead of just telling me I was great, and everything would be fine (which they also did), they asked me to describe the best outcome. I talked about standing at the podium with confidence and giving a speech that made my classmates cheer, and, better still, vote for me.

"Keep imagining that," my parents said, *"and you'll do fine."*

I can't tell you that I didn't have another negative thought before Friday's assembly, but whenever I did I would repeat in my mind the positive outcome I desired. On that Friday, I did indeed stand up with confidence, share the improvements I wanted to make at the school, and I won!

From that, I reached two conclusions: First, it helps to imagine the best outcome. Second, strong passion overcomes nerves.

Twenty years later I find myself helping people improve their lives every day as a transformation consultant. One day I was reminded of that grade school incident as I was leaving the stage after speaking to a group of professionals looking for help living their ideal life.

The thing that stood out to me, as I finished up interacting with the people who had come up to the stage to talk to me that day was, that my true passion is not only to help people, but to find more ways to reach everybody I want to help.

At the same time, it struck me that along my own journey, I've realized that I can't give to others what I don't have myself.

It's the analogy about putting the oxygen mask on yourself before helping someone else. As I encourage people to unleash their full potential, I check in with myself to make sure I am living to my fullest potential in all areas of my life.

It's a dynamic pursuit in that we change as we grow, as we learn new skills, and as our interests change. At one point in time, improving my life focused on my health, career and social life. As time went by, the picture of a better life now includes my marriage, parenthood and my community.

Early in my career, I reflected on my life, which, like everyone else's, was full of highs, lows and plateaus. I wondered if I could codify what allowed for my successes, failures, and the moments when I just seemed to be living without much intention. Thinking about my grade school experience and my life since, I was reminded that every situation where I achieved my greatest success I had an ideal picture in my head—and I didn't have one when I fell short or fell into complacency.

Over the years I've studied great leaders, coaches, parents, and partners that I had the opportunity to be around to discover if they knew intuitively what I understood and was sharing in my presentations: Thinking in ideals can bring it into being.

I've found again and again that a strong trait shared by self- help gurus like Lou Tice, great coaches like John Wooden, social change leaders like Mother Teresa, Ghandi and Martin Luther King Jr., and spiritual leaders like the Dalai Lama and Desmond Tutu was the ability to see things how they wanted them to be and to hold on to that picture despite the current circumstances.

That brings me to this book. Over the past 15 years I've traveled around the world talking to people about how to fully unleash their potential. Sometimes the audience is full of CEOs or senior leaders, sometimes athletic coaches, other times educators, parents and young people. I also spoke with inmates at prison—talk about a captive audience who wants a more ideal life!

Typically what follows my presentation is a line of people who gather at the front of the venue and want to carry on the conversation, so great is their desire to share their story and get more information that would allow them to immediately apply some of the lessons to their own lives.

They all ask the same question, "How do I make things better?"-- "things" being their marriage, job, happiness, health, [insert what you want here]. We all pretty much want something in our life to change, and the skills to make it happen.

I want to help. If our conversation was too short, or maybe we haven't even met but you want more about how to live your ideal life, I want to share information that will get you closer to it, and maybe all the way there.

When I first sat down to write this book, I thought, *"What is the #1 reason that people don't live their best life? Why aren't they the best they can be in their personal lives, relationships, families, community, business or profession, health, finances— or whatever is important where they live?"*

I'm not the first person to write about the reasons, circumstances and characteristics that keep us from reaching our potential. What I can also add is a blueprint to help you create the Ideal picture of your life. To do that, we have to flip the question.

Rather than focus on what holds us back, I want to focus on what allows us to soar.

The goal of this book is to share the information and actions you can take to identify your potential, help you recognize what's keeping you from living your best life, and set you on a path to achieve your ideal outcomes.

I'll talk about the characteristics successful people have in common-- traits like a strong work ethic, rituals, and positive attitudes. Successful people are option thinkers, optimistic, and don't mind the hard work of change. I'll share how each one of them learned or knew intuitively the importance of thinking in Ideals.

This book covers three phases: 1) Thinking in Ideals, 2) Breaking Through Barriers That Prevent Us from Our Ideal, and

3) Realizing Your Ideal Outcomes. Along the way, I'll tell you the reasons you should think in Ideals, backed by research, stories from thousands of people around the world that I've talked to, and my own experience realizing Ideals in every area of my life.

First up, why I think we are wired for success when it comes to thinking in Ideals.

Phase 1

A JOURNEY TO HAPPINESS AND FULFILMENT

Chapter 1

Why it's Important to Think in Ideals

There is a story of two architects who were bidding on a contract. Both architects submitted beautiful, elegant, breathtaking designs of what they would build. In fact, the designs were both so amazing that the client who had commissioned the plans soon found themself unable to decide which design they liked better. They asked each architect to present their design to the Board of Trustees after which they would decide who would be granted the contract.

The first architect gave an impressive presentation on his inspiration for the design. He discussed the complex structure yet simple form, the materials he would use, and the state- of- the-art technology that he'd designed into the building. He covered every detail—right down to the screws that would be used. It was clear that he had thought about everything. At the end of his presentation, the Trustees only asked him one question:

"If we needed to make some budget cuts, what would you do?"

The architect then explained why he believed he shouldn't change anything as it was stunning and a game-changer for building design. After he finished, the Trustees thought that there was no way that the second architect could top the first architect's presentation and that, at most, they would still be deadlocked.

The second architect came in and stood at the front of the room. She asked the Trustees to go on a journey, and with that she shared her vision. She began by describing not the building itself, but, rather, how it would improve the functional experience of real people. She described people entering and leaving the building, interacting with the space and each other as they did. Then she looked out five, 10, 20 years in the future and described what the building would become in the community. After the architect shared her vision, she explained the details of the building design.

When she was done, the Trustees asked her the same question they had asked the first architect. This time they got a different response. The architect said that the most important factor was the purpose the building would

serve. She told the Trustees that the ideal picture was not in the materials but how the building worked for people. She explained that as long as the Trustees held on to the ideal image of the building, she could find ways to turn out that image.

The second architect won the contract and went on to build it.

I believe that we are all architects of our own future. But how many of us start with an ideal picture of what we want to build in each area of our life? How we want it to function?

Interact with other parts of our lives?

I've spoken to thousands of people all over the world and what I've found is that most people think in terms of what they believe is possible or what they think is reasonable. But what's true is that what motivates us—what gives us the energy to overcome obstacles, to take on giants, and to endure hardship is the strong driver that only resides in the Ideal picture.

I've also found that most people have never been told about the power and importance of thinking in Ideals.

My whole life I'd been goal setting. The problem was goal setting didn't guarantee goal getting. And I wasn't alone. Research shows that only 8 percent of people achieve their goals. It wasn't until I was in my mid-20s that I was taught the importance and skill of setting Ideal goals and thinking about Ideal outcomes that I want in my life.

I was invited to attend a workshop by Lou Tice, founder of the Pacific

Institute and renowned self-help and leadership development guru (Lou became one of my mentors and a trusted friend). At the time, I was the youngest VP of Sales for a large national company. I had a company car, a home office, and a large upscale office that I rarely visited in downtown Seattle, Wash. I was engaged to the most wonderful woman, who is now my wife. On all counts, life was amazing!

During the workshop, Lou asked this question multiple times, "Is this what you want? Is this what's ideal (for your family life, your health, your community, your work, your spiritual life, and more)?" It hit me that, even though life was amazing, it wasn't ideal. What's more, I hadn't really thought about what would be ideal; I just knew I was happy with how things were going.

I hadn't thought about my ideal job; I just knew I wanted to be successful. I hadn't thought about an ideal marriage; I just knew I wanted to be married to this incredible woman. I hadn't thought about what was ideal for making a difference in my community; I just knew that I wanted to be involved.

Lou's question got me thinking.

I started to study the greatest achievers, many of whom are my heroes or mentors and all of whom have mastered the power of Ideals. The great basketball player Michael Jordan visualized the ideal outcome of a last-second shot. Steve Jobs, the mastermind behind the Apple computer, thought about the ideal impact of turning technology into tools that were easy to use, that helped people realize their dreams and changed the world for the better. And civil rights activist Martin Luther King Jr. shared his ideal dream for a world that seemed so far away.

The key is defining your Ideal. If you could describe a perfect outcome, one that meets your personal sense of excellence, what would it be? Throughout this book, I'll be asking you that question.

This isn't, "think it and it will come to you." Ideal goals aren't easy to achieve. But if you start thinking of Ideals, your life will move in that direction. And you don't have to take my word for it. Studies show the importance of thinking in ideals. Let me share with you the reasons you don't have to settle for "possible" and "reasonable" when you can have Ideal.

Reason #1: We Move Toward What We Think

Did you know that you are teleological? Before you object, let me explain. The word "teleological" is derived from two Greek words, Telos (meaning end, goal or purpose) and Logos (meaning reason or explanation) and it means to think in terms of the purpose of things, rather than their cause. The philosophy of teleology is better left to philosophers and really smart biologists, but simply put, it means that we move towards what we think about. Psychological research has shown that humans think in pictures and are drawn towards the pictures that we hold in our minds. This happens whether that picture is good for you or not; you're drawn to it either way.

Have you ever had this happen: You notice something on the floor and think, "Don't trip on that..," and sure enough you trip on it? Or, "Don't spill your wine on the white table cloth..," and minutes later, oops, there you go? Why? Because you put the picture of tripping and spilling in your head and subconsciously you are drawn toward what you think about. It's the reason that when people are learning to ride a motorcycle they're instructed to always look at where they want to go because they will subconsciously steer the bike in that direction.

Since we move toward what we think about, it stands to reason that it's important to think about what we want instead of what we don't want. Another important piece to this: The mind receives no picture from the word "Don't." Anytime we use that word, the mind completely bypasses it. Tell a child, "Don't touch the___," and no more than

two minutes later they will be reaching for that very thing. The same thing happens when someone tells you to not turn around--your impulse is to turn around. Because we move toward what we think about. Now that you know this, when it comes to the areas of our life that we care about, can you see how important it is to think about the ideal picture or the ideal outcome? Knowing that we move toward what we think about, why would we spend time thinking about what we *don't* want or even what would be *nice*, rather than thinking about what would be Ideal?

When my sister and I were young, my parents would take us on family vacations every summer. After returning from the family vacation, my parents would also take a vacation just by themselves (they probably needed a vacation from the family vacation). While that seemed unfair to my young mind, they always brought us something back, which let us know that while they were away, they were still thinking of us. While we couldn't wait for them to get back, more precisely, we also couldn't wait for them to unpack.

Normally, I got a t-shirt from the location or a cool souvenir. When I was 10-years-old, I got something different.

My Dad handed me a big piece of cardboard.

On the other side was a poster of a large house and fancy cars, by a beach. In the perfect-blue sky was printed the motivational message: *Justification for a Higher Education*.

I didn't have a clue what the words meant, but I liked the picture. At this age I was really into cars and loved playing with model cars of Lamborghinis and Ferraris. I was psyched about all of the beautiful cars on this poster. My dad then sat me down and clarified that "higher education" meant college. It was a brilliant move! He connected "higher education" to something that he knew interested me at the time. I hung the poster in my room and for the rest of the eight years I lived at home, I looked at that poster every day.

When my dad gave me the poster, did I know what *Justification for a Higher Education* meant? Nope. Did I set the goal to go to college when

I hung it on the wall? No again. But as I grew up, as I made plans, I liked what I saw in the poster. Message received: Higher Education is the key. If cars and beach houses were cool, then college had to be part of my picture. I'd say that the poster got me thinking, and moving toward college. College got me closer to my reaching my potential and achieving my Ideal. You can say it was like my first vision board. While in college my idea of what success looks like matured and it was no longer about cars. I realized that my Ideal picture was about helping others and helping my community and so I changed the "poster" and as I move through life I continue to change or add to the "poster" all of the time.

Think about your life and what you would like to improve. Even if your life is good, think of one area you would like to move from good to great. Take a moment and write that area down.

*1 Area I want to improve:*_____

Chapter 2

Igniting the Drive

A few years ago, I was working in Los Angeles with NFL coach Pete Carrol's A Better L.A. project, which is a non-profit organization that works with inner city youth to solve problems in their community by giving them the tools and resources to lead change. There was a partnership between A Better L.A. and the City to create a program called Summer Night Lights. The program was designed to address the violence that was taking place in and around the parks throughout the city. The strategy was to hire young people in the community and empower them to create safe programs and activities. My job was to help train the youth workers on "mindset," which is to say, I was there to help them see this as an opportunity and learning experience. Big shift since the prevailing culture was one of believing there wasn't much they could do to improve things and to try was to risk being held up for scrutiny and judgment.

I arrived and got to work organizing 40 young people between the ages of 16-20-years old. I'm working my magic, introducing myself, sharing my story and thinking I'm going to inspire them to do this great work.

At some point I notice that the group is constantly describing how bad the situation is. And it is bad. I heard stories about people not being able to go beyond a four- block radius of where they lived because of a very real fear of violence.

Several people had lost a loved one to violence—including one young man whose brother had been shot and killed two days before the workshop. It was all very real and very important for them to have a place to talk about the daily horrors. At the same time, it was clear to me that they were only talking about the problems and weren't thinking about any solutions.

Tony was a perfect example. He stood up in one group meeting and went off about how the meeting and the project was all a big waste of time. He asked the candid question, "How can we convince other people that the parks would be safe, when we know for a fact that they aren't?"

When he was finished, I walked over to the white board and picked up a dry erase marker. Turning to the whole group, I asked "What do you want for your community?" That was why we were there, right? --to find solutions to problems in their neighborhood, but we'd gotten stuck just talking about the problems and not the Ideal. That single question, "What do you want for your community?" changed everything.

At first, the group sat there in silence. I could see them thinking it through. Finally, someone said, "I don't know that we've ever been asked that before."

"What would make this an ideal place to live?" I asked.

Someone said, "...a movie theater," then someone said, "we need a grocery store." Someone said, "... a clean park," then someone said, "jobs," and someone added, "...job training" for the people in the neighborhood so that they got the jobs.

Ideas were coming at me rapid fire and I was having a hard time keeping up. The energy in the room had completely shifted as the group co-created the Ideal picture of their community.

At the end of the brainstorming session I asked the group how they felt, and the answer moved me to my core. "I feel like we can actually do this," Tony said. "Now I understand the importance of this summer job."

Reason #2: We Tend to Get Stuck

As people, we tend to get stuck. We find ourselves in a rut sometimes without even knowing we're in one because even in a rut, we keep going. What does a rut feel like? You're not really looking forward to anything.

The flip side of getting stuck is setting a goal and going for it.

Have you ever set a goal, thought about it day and night and then worked hard until you accomplished that goal? Maybe it's to run a marathon, open a restaurant, or change jobs. You start getting up earlier to run, you start looking at real estate or doing research online. Isn't it amazing how much energy and creativity you have once you've set a goal?

Whether we finish our goal or not, what happens next is that we stop. Unless we set another goal, we can find ourselves in kind of a holding pattern. We look up three years later and realize that things haven't changed much since we started, stopped, or completed the goal we'd set for ourselves. Our rut then is just maintaining the current state of things. We get comfortable with our life.

But what if you are not living the life you want? What if you want more?

I was having breakfast once with Dr. Tamebechi, a leading psychologist in Japan, and considered by many to be one of the greatest minds of our time. I asked him how to help people get out of a rut. Dr. T responded with something that was so simple and deeply profound. He said, "The best way to help people let go of their past or where they currently are is to help them fall in love with their future."

That statement stuck with me as if he'd shouted it in my ear from close range. How simple! But, as someone once told me, "simple isn't always easy."

What's true is that thinking in Ideals helps you fall in love with your future. It's about creating a future that is so Ideal in your mind that you can't stand not seeing it realized. A picture that is so filled with positive outcomes that you find yourself thinking about it all the time.

The same thing happens when we fall in love with someone or something. We think about that person or item all the time. We attach happiness to their photo or to memories of activities we did together, and we imagine the wonderful things we will do. That's what we need to do for our lives.

We need to take the time to create pictures of our future that are so beautiful that we fall in love with it.

That's what Tony and the other young people in the Summer Night Lights program did. They fell in love with the new picture of their neighborhood. The picture was so beautiful that they were excited to put in the work to make it a reality. You don't change culture overnight and turn years of neglect on its head right away, but Tony and the others moved toward a desired future reality that summer, and L.A. had its safest summer in more than 40 years.

I remember when I fell in love with my wife. Not only did I think about her every day, but I found myself thinking of all the days ahead. At first it was just thinking about where I might take her on a date, but as I fell deeper in love and I knew I wanted to ask her to marry me, I started thinking about how and where I would propose. When I imagined my Ideal life, she was in it, and still today she's part of it every time and all the time. Even as I write this, the very thought of her makes my heart smile. I'd gladly take time from something else to spend time with her. We all deserve to fall in love with our future—with all areas of life, and especially with people that make it Ideal.

What is something you have fallen in love with? _____

How did it make you feel? _____

16

Reason #3: Your Brain is Ready to Give You What You Need

You might have gathered from Reason #2 that thinking in Ideals releases passion! Our brains like goal setting. Anytime you set a goal, your brain releases energy, spurs creativity, and expands your awareness to find what you need to accomplish the goal.

Back to our example of setting a goal to run a marathon, open a restaurant, or change jobs. When the goal is set correctly, our brains will release enough energy to train, research, apply—do whatever is required.

The good and bad thing about it is that the brain will always release just enough energy to accomplish the goal, but only enough energy to reach the goal, and that's it.

That's why you'll find yourself staying up late or waking up early to workout but once you've run the marathon, you go back to your normal sleep schedule. As soon as you cross that finish line, it's like someone flipped the light switch off. Our brains tell our bodies how much energy to release based on what is required to reach the goal, and the moment that the goal is accomplished the brain shuts off and goes into conservation mode.

The same thing happens when you're close to finishing a project and you're tired, but you tell yourself, "Five more minutes, just give me five more minutes to get it done," and your body gives you five minutes. But as soon as the timer runs out on five minutes, game over. You hit the "Done" or "Send" button and Zap, just like that, your energy is gone.

The same goes for creativity and awareness. Your brain will give you just enough ideas to help you accomplish your goal. You will figure out how you can fit in time to train, how you can squeeze in a drive past a building for lease or adjust your other activities to take a course that adds a new skill to your resume.

Your brain seems to get excited that you've set a goal and starts finding ways for you to accomplish it. If it's time you need, you find it. If it's an available space for your restaurant, a space opens up. A new job? A recruiter calls you. Once again though, you get just enough to help you accomplish your goal.

I'd also have you remember this: Small goals, small energy, creativity and awareness. Big goals, big energy, creativity, and awareness. So why not set a big goal? In fact, set the Ideal goal! Your mind and body will release all the energy, creativity and awareness you need. If it's going to give you what you need, you might as well think about what you truly want, Ideally.

Reason #4: We Get What We Expect

In 2008, Lou Tice and Mark Schubert (the then coach of the

U.S. Olympic Swim Team) invited me to work with members of the U.S. Olympic swim team. They had just come back from Beijing where the team had won a total of 31 medals to maintain the U.S.'s standing as the most successful nation in swimming.

I was talking to them about thinking in Ideals, being teleological, and setting goals. If ever there is a group of people who set goals, it's competitive athletes!

I also introduced the fact that we often get what we expect.

This concept is sometimes referred to as the "sure enough" principle. You've also heard it referred to as the self-fulfilling prophecy. Expect a bad day, and chances are you'll have one. Expect a good day, and chances are you'll have one. Henry Ford said it best, "Whether you think you can, or you think you can't—you're right." By thinking in Ideals, we are raising the level of what we expect and are drawn in that direction.

One of the swimmers shouted out, "Oh my God! I so just did this to myself!" She went on to explain how she had set a goal to make it on to the U.S. swim team and go to the Olympics in 2008. Every day, she trained, in and out of the pool. It was hard work but getting on the team made it worth it. She swam in Beijing but didn't medal. What she realized was that her goal needed to be bigger. She'd set a goal to make it to the Olympics, but her Ideal goal was to win a medal.

Speed forward to 2012, I'm back working with the swim team, right after they'd competed in the Olympics in London. The same swimmer. Different goal and different results. This time, she'd set a goal to be on the team AND medal, and she'd accomplished her goals, winning a silver and a bronze.

Her response? "I forgot to set the goal to win the gold; I only set the goal to medal!"

If you're going to set goals, set them based on your Ideal picture and the best outcome because chances are you'll move toward it, release enough energy, creativity and awareness to achieve it, and overcome any obstacles that land in your path.

Reason #5: Ideals Make Us Happy

Who doesn't want to be happy?

If I told you that thinking in Ideals makes you happy, wouldn't you get onboard? End of chapter?

Why don't more of us think in Ideals if doing it will make us happy?

Because while we all say we want to be happy, a lot of us haven't really defined what happiness looks like. Without defining it, we live our life and call it "good." Or good enough. But we can't say it's Ideal.

I was sitting in traffic and thinking about the amount of stress that people are under. All the decisions that need to be made in a person's day. The (im)balance of work and life. The homework that needs to get graded, the bills that have to be paid, the employees that need our attention. The list can go on and on. I'm thinking about all this while I'm on I-5 going nowhere fast and I asked myself this question,

"Why do all of this work for a life that isn't even Ideal for me?"

At the time, I had that great job I mentioned before. It paid me well, with amazing benefits. I had a company car, and I could choose to work from home or my really nice office in downtown Seattle. I had a company phone and company credit card. I was covered. I was also happy, for the most part. From a distance, this was an ideal situation and it almost was, except for the fact that I wasn't fulfilled.

Happiness and fulfilment are different. Happiness is a range of emotions from satisfaction to joy that come from recognizing and appreciating what's good in your life. Fulfilment is a deeper sense of joy and satisfaction—even peace, when you feel you are truly doing what you were created to do or doing what you pictured in your own mind as ideal. Fulfillment really deals with passion and thoughtful design.

I've known for a long time that one of the things that fulfills me is helping others unleash their full potential. The job with all the perks? Awesome, but it wasn't my Ideal. I wasn't feeling satisfaction but I was very happy. I also didn't think I was maxing out my potential or doing what I was meant to do. I wasn't *fulfilled.*

Around the same time, I had the opportunity to travel to Guatemala and conduct a two-day workshop that would help other people tap into their potential. On the plane ride home, it hit me—and you'll appreciate the irony of me thinking this on an airplane: I needed to put the oxygen mask on myself first.

How could I teach others to think in Ideals and reach their potential, when I wasn't doing it myself?

I opened my laptop and began to ask and answer the question, "What would be Ideal for me?"

I was typing things like, "working with people on unleashing their potential," "overcoming obstacles," "problem solving/solution finding," "traveling around the world," "making my own schedule." The more I kept at it, the more specific I got and I was able to clarify that I wanted to "work with diverse groups from corporations, non-profits, education, athletics, and young people, to help them define and achieve their Ideal life."

Something magical happened as I typed that statement. I could see my Ideal. I was imagining doing all that work and I was excited. I felt like I was unburying gold. And I began to fall in love with my Ideal job.

Within the next few months, I left my job and started my consulting firm, Potential Unleashed Consulting. That was more than 10 years ago!

Have there been bumps and bruises along the way? Absolutely. Were there obstacles and setbacks? A few. Was I scared? Excited? Yes, and yes. But I kept referring to the image of my Ideal and taking the necessary steps to achieve my goals. Knowing that I was working toward my Ideal made the work fun because I wasn't just thinking of Ideals, I was working toward them. And I was happier than I'd ever been in any of the other jobs I'd had.

I believe thinking in Ideals is life changing. Why? Because it works for me. More importantly, it works for a lot of people, and I believe it will work for you too.

It starts by asking and answering one question for every part of your life.

What is your Ideal?

What is Ideal for your marriage? What is Ideal for raising your children? What is your ideal home for your family? What is Ideal for your business? What is Ideal for your community?

What is Ideal for your relationships and friendships? What's Ideal for your health?

It's a simple question and putting it out there has enormous impact. You can encourage others to answer the question too. I ask my children all the time. I ask my daughters and they will tell me what Ideal is for their birthday parties, for their performance in the school play, for today at school. What I've found is, asking the question increases the likelihood that everybody gets what they imagined or dreamed of.

Practice It

Pick something simple from your life that will happen in the next 2 Or 3 days (a dinner, lunch, meeting, weekend activity, etc.)

_____

What would be Ideal for this situation?

What is the scene? _____

Who is present? _____

What is the desired outcome? _____

How do you want to feel? _____

Chapter 3

Attracting Opportunities

Have you heard of the idea of "out of sight, out of mind?" It means that we stop thinking about something or someone if we don't think of or see that thing or person for a period. It's a sure-fire way to make sure something doesn't get our attention and that bad things don't happen to us.

I want to talk about making sure good things happen for us.

One of the things that stops us from getting our goals is not having an image of the Ideal in your head. In other words, "out of mind, out of sight." If you're not regularly thinking about the results you want, chances are that you won't see the gifts around you that could help you accomplish that goal.

Years ago, I was given an assignment to take a look at my life and write down what I wanted when I was older.

A second part of the assignment was to write down what I wanted to accomplish in the next 12 months. Like everyone else, I wrote down things I wanted like happiness, money, a good job, a relationship. But the instructions were to be specific, so I went into detail, including what I intended to accomplish in the next year. You know I love this stuff, so I kept the paper and referred to it throughout the year. In the next 12 months, I accomplished most of what I'd written down and was on my way to achieving what I wanted later on.

And then I lost track of the paper.

Years later, I found it. Good for me, I had accomplished most of what was on the paper. But if I'd had the paper in front of me, if I'd kept it in my wallet or taped it on to my bathroom mirror, I think I would have completed more and done it faster. I also realized that on my paper, I hadn't been specific enough. "Settle down," isn't as strong as "meet strong, empowered woman who shares my same values and interests." I checked the box on being in a relationship, but it wasn't my Ideal relationship. I'd written down that I wanted a high-paying job. Got that, but as I mentioned earlier, it was less than Ideal too.

When you're setting goals, be specific. Also revisit your goals and look for new opportunities, especially if what you get isn't Ideal.

A friend of mine was working for a large corporation when the Great Recession hit in 2008. My friend was laid off but was lucky to get a good severance package. I invited him out to dinner, to check in on how he was feeling about his circumstances. I assumed he was anxious and uncertain about what to do next. At dinner, I asked him what his plan was for moving forward. He said that because of his severance, he really wasn't in a rush to the "next thing."

He had time to think in Ideals.

He thought about the Ideal job, then the Ideal industry, the Ideal company, the Ideal leadership, the Ideal culture, the Ideal structure within the organization, the Ideal compensation, the Ideal location—his list got very specific. When he had a clear picture in his mind, he looked online for jobs and contacted his network of friends. People started calling him with opportunities. He got two offers with companies that matched his Ideal image. Case in point: Thinking in Ideals is not only like a magnet that draws you to it, it attracts more opportunities to you as well.

Research shows that there is so much going on around us all of the time that our brains actually build blind spots to information that it regards as unimportant. It's the brain's way of protecting us and helping us to focus.

The trick is to remind yourself of the Ideal, perhaps just a single sentence, that tells your brain it's important. Your statement will clue your brain in advance what to look for throughout the day.

Have you ever thought about going on a vacation to a place that you have never visited? Maybe you've seen an ad and then discussed it with someone you know who has vacationed there before. Once you decide to go to that location for your next vacation, an amazing thing happens. Information about that location will crop up everywhere. The person in front of you at the grocery store will be wearing a shirt from that place. Someone at work will share a story about their vacation there. Your screensaver will have a picture of the place in its rotation.

Coincidence? Not at all. Once you set the goal and commit to that goal, your brain opens up to find information about that place or thing. Why does this happen? Because you set the goal. Your brain likes goals and gives goals more attention, making it easier for you to get what you want.

Thinking in Ideals is like planning that vacation.

The things we want in our life are already all around us; we're just not seeing or hearing them. When you set a goal, you give new importance to information and tell your brain to see exactly what you tell it you want.

At this point, many of you are thinking, "I've set goals, and nothing has shown itself to me!" You're wondering where all the help I say is there for you is hiding.

It's waiting for an Ideal goal.

You see, small goals don't excite people. All the things on your To Do List? Low on the Importance Scale to anybody but you. People get jazzed about Ideal goals more than small goals.

That doesn't mean that the goal has to be huge. What it lacks in size, it can make up for by having a beautiful, meaningful story behind it.

Reason #6: There's Power in Sharing

"If you want to build a ship, don't drum up people to collect wood and don't assign them tasks and work, teach them to long for the endless immensity of the sea."

This is one of my favorite quotes and it explains really well the sixth reason we should think in Ideals. When you draw others into your Ideal pictures you unleash the passion and energy in their brains too. There is something about the Ideal that attracts other people to it, and by association, to you. The world loves a visionary (we also call them dreamers, and, most importantly strong leaders).

I've coached a lot of leaders. Good leaders share their Ideal vision for the future all the time. Big, bold, wild Ideals. The best leaders paint a really vivid picture. They articulate it in a way that gets their audience to really believe it can be true. They use inspiring, passionate words. Steve Jobs stirred up people's enthusiasm by saying, "Let's make a dent in the Universe!'

When others connect to your exciting vision for the future, they also connect their energy, passion, creativity, and expanded awareness to it. If you follow it up with strong habits, a sensible approach and reasonable assumptions, then everyone will be convinced that your ideal will really happen and support it.

President John F. Kennedy's visit to NASA is a good example of the power of sharing Ideals. The story has many versions, so I'll share my favorite.

In 1962, JFK visited the NASA Launch Operations Center. This was a year after he had given a speech to a joint session of Congress that set the U.S. on a course to the moon.

During the visit, JFK noticed a janitor carrying a broom. He interrupted his tour to introduce himself to the man. "Hi, I'm Jack Kennedy. What are you doing?"

"Well, Mr. President," the janitor responded, "I'm helping put a man on the moon." When we set Ideal goals and share them with others, we connect with people by reminding them that great things can be achieved.

A huge issue organizations often have is inspiring people. I was coaching an executive who had shared with me how disappointed he was that his employees seemed disengaged. Human Resources had suggested a lot of things they could do to get people pumped up. Pizza parties, beer on Fridays, latte machines, stuff like that. None of it seemed to have a lasting effect. Employees would eat, drink and be merry but then everything seemed to go back to business as usual. More concerning, the executive wasn't seeing any innovative ideas coming from the organization. People seemed to be watching the clock closer than ever, and he couldn't remember a time recently when someone had done anything outside of their regular scope of work, either for the customer or their colleagues.

"What can we do to reignite the fire?" the executive asked me. "I want my employees engaged. I want them bringing their ideas to our meetings, collaborating with each other and strengthening our company. How do I shift our culture to get that?"

I really try not to answer a question with another question, but I did in this case.

"You just told me what the Ideal culture would be," I said, "but where does this company want to be in 10, even 50 years?"

You see, over the years and with all of the changes that every company goes through, his company had lost sight of the higher meaning and purpose of its work.

Instead of hiring people to do a job, find people who have a passion for what they do and then inspire them with it to bring their passion to help you "put a man on the moon."

Good leaders have a vision for the future and enlist others to support it. They imagine great opportunities ahead, and they develop an Ideal image of the future that benefits a lot of people. They are good communicators and their vision is simple, clear, exciting, and smart. Their ability to articulate, persuade, or engage can have powerful results, including a boost in competitiveness and a positive impact on the bottom line.

How? By getting people to add their passion, energy and creativity to accomplishing the goal, the dream or the movement. In contrast, having a vague idea without specific details can have immediate and devastating consequences.

People choose to follow people who can share their vision, express their passion for it, and create a cause for commitment (why people should care). When people can feel a leader's energy, they will add their energy to the goal, and even come up with creative ways to achieve the Ideal because we all want to achieve something great.

The same applies to your personal goals. Your ideal image doesn't have to be around growing a company to a billion dollars or solving the war in Syria. It can be about creating a better world for yourself and your family. There have been many times in my life when people have helped me or jumped into a cause I believe in. My wife has helped me manifest all types of ideas. I've also been blessed to attract and connect with people like Mike Seifert, LaDonte King, Noah Prince, Dr. Jennifer Jimenez and others to our team. Without them, much of our success would not have happened the way it did. Our Ideal pictures for the world matched and created amazing synergy.

It's almost like magic.

Once you know what you truly want, your image is vivid and clear, and you share that with others and talk about how they can make a difference, people will begin to pop up out of nowhere with opportunities for you to move toward that picture. It's not magic, but it is powerful.

Phase 2

BREAKING THROUGH BARRIERS
THAT HOLD US BACK

Chapter 4

The #1 Barrier is Fear

I was five-years-old when I watched Nightmare on Elm Street for the first time. I know what you are thinking, "Why in the world would your parents allow you to do that?" In their defense, my parents didn't know. I was sleeping over at a friend's house and his older sister allowed us to watch the movie with her and her friends. Even at five-years-old, my friend and I wanted to prove that we were brave and tough, and we sat through the entire movie.

Bad idea.

Afterwards, we couldn't sleep. As the night wore on and we wore out, we negotiated back and forth who should go to sleep first because we knew we couldn't both sleep at the same time.

The problem with watching the movie at that age is that we couldn't separate fiction from reality. We really believed that Freddy Kruger was going to get us as soon as we closed our eyes. It never occurred to us that if Freddy were real, he'd probably have come for us long before now, as well as the Hollywood producers who'd made a movie about him.

I was still terrified the next day and told my family. They weren't pleased with my friend's sister, although my uncle thought it was pretty funny. The next time my parents went out and left him to watch me, he taped knives to his fingers, put on a fedora hat, and stood in the hallway, tapping the walls outside my bedroom. This was terrifying to me on a new level. Now, not only was Freddy real, he knew where I lived.

Wait, it gets worse.

I usually had to go to the bathroom in the middle of the night. Some nights, I had to go a couple of times, and the bathroom was on the other side of the hallway. Out of habit and good fiscal management, my parents turned off all the lights in the house at night. Now imagine five-year-old Jahmad willing his bladder to "hold it" as long as possible, and then getting up the courage to dash for my life, running out of my bedroom and leaping across the hallway into the bathroom (I also believed that jumping made me faster and if I was in the air, Freddy couldn't touch me. Remember, five-year-old logic).

Is that silly? Of course, it is.

But fear is a powerful force. It replaces logic and takes control of our actions. It can also paralyze us and prevent us from taking any action at all. If I could have stayed awake and not gone to the bathroom ever, I would have, rather than risk facing what I was afraid of.

The #1 barrier to people thinking in terms of Ideals is fear. More than being motivated to make good things happen for them, they are driven to make sure bad things don't happen to them. They're so afraid that bad things are around the corner that they take the first good thing that comes along and hold on to it for dear life. They wanted a job; they got a job. Good enough. They wanted a relationship; they're in a relationship, and good or bad, they're sticking with that person. It doesn't matter if what they have is not Ideal, it's something and they're done. They are so concerned with doing without that they don't allow themselves to visualize having more.

Remember the concept of being teleological and the fact that we move toward what we think about? Fear either keeps us from moving forward or moves us to a state that is far short of Ideal.

When we were Neanderthals, fear was a useful tool for survival. If we saw a wooly mammoth charging us, fear ignited the fight or flight response and helped us stay alive. The problem is, fear still causes the same biological response even though the mammoths are extinct and we face far fewer life- threatening situations.

The good news about fear is that you can overcome it. But first you must recognize it.

How can you tell when fear is at play? When I ask someone what they want and they begin by telling me what they don't want, fear has the upper hand.

Recognizing fear is a big step forward toward realizing your Ideal. Listen for it, understanding that fear is sneaky and subtle. It can look like mindfulness or thinking through contingencies, but it's fear parading itself as perfectly good reasons why you shouldn't reach for your Ideal.

When you go to set a goal, visualize a new reality or dream in the Ideal, and start to say, "That will never work," or ask, "What if they say 'No,'? or "What if she fires me?" "What if they laugh?" "What if I can't do it?" that's fear talking.

Dr. Albert Bandura, social psychology professor emeritus at Stanford University, says, "Fear is the root cause of all dysfunction." Read that again. Fear is the root cause of all dysfunction.

"Dysfunction" is defined as when people know what to do but they still don't do it (as opposed to ignorance, which is when we don't know what to do). I can tell you that you can live an Ideal life, but fear will prevent you from getting started, no matter how many success stories, tips and scientific facts I give you.

As you start to recognize fear, it's helpful to understand the biological and psychological forces behind it. Fear creates stress on the body, which releases cortisol. Cortisol is a stress hormone designed to protect you against perceived threats. It generally gets released along with adrenaline. When these hormones are triggered and released in the body unnecessarily—or constantly, because you live in fear and stress, they become toxins that can put you at higher risk for health problems and disease.

How do we get beyond fear? Here are some things that I have learned over time and apply to my own life.

I'm a little different when it comes to fear. I seek it out. Is that strange? A little. Let me explain.

I'm always practicing the principal of thinking in ideals. I set goals or take on new tasks that are often way outside my comfort zone. It's like telling fear, "I'll leave the light on for you." And fear checks in, every time. Maybe not right away because sometimes the initial excitement of taking on a new challenge is bigger than the fear, but somewhere down the road fear pops in for a visit.

Knowing this, I try to get the fear out of the way first. I know it's there, lurking, and waiting to catch me off guard. It's playing a game of cat and mouse.

Rather than let fear sneak up on me, I go hunting for it. I'd much rather face it when I am prepared, so that I can confront it, fight it and defeat it on my own terms.

Here are four things I do:

First, I define what I really want. This sounds easier than it is. I'll talk more about this in Phase 3.

Second, I identify what I'm afraid will happen when I go after what I want.

Normally when we think of fear, we think of it as a feeling. When something scares us, we get an emotional hit to our system followed by all types of symptoms such as sweaty palms, shaky legs, and butterflies in the stomach. Those are the natural emotional and biological response to fear. But remember I said that fear was sneaky. It likes to disguise itself. It will parade excuses in front of you disguised as perfectly good reasons not to do something. "I'm too busy," "there's just not enough time," "it probably isn't that good of an idea anyway," are all fear talking.

36

When we identify fear as fear, and not good reasons, we can treat it for what it is. Once I identify what I'm afraid of, I can rise above it. You can literally say, "Fear, I hear you saying that I am too busy to take on this project, but I'm not going to listen to you today." If you don't take on fear like that, it only gets bigger and stronger.

Third, I isolate fear. The truth is that I'm probably not afraid of the entire goal, dream, task, or Ideal; most often it's only a small piece of it that causes me to be afraid. But fear is like a little dog with an incessant yap. It likes to make itself look bigger.

My friend has talked for years about wanting to advance his career. To do that, he would have to go back to school for his Master's degree. Whenever I ask him if he's enrolled in a program, he tells me what's holding him back. Usually it's, "this isn't the right time."

I asked him again when he was at my house for a BBQ. He came out to the deck where I was cooking and asked if he could help.

I fancy myself to be a bit of a Pit Master. A real Grill Guy. I usually have two grills going at the same time. So, I said, "Sure. You can help me keep an eye on that grill, while I handle this one and go back-and-forth to the kitchen to prep."

Normally I would never let someone be in charge of my grill, but I took this opportunity to cook up a Life Lesson as well. While we were at the grills, I asked him again about his career goals and whether he still wanted to get his Masters.

The first thing out of his mouth was, "Yes, but...." followed by the same old excuses. I asked him what he was afraid of.

After a long silence, he said, "The truth is, I'm scared to go back to school. It's been a long time since I was in college and even then, I wasn't a great student. What if it's too hard?"

Bingo! Fear had attached itself to getting a graduate degree and made itself even bigger with memories of his last experience at college.

I reminded him of how much he had grown since college. He was smart, capable and had good time management skills, all of which I said would set him up well to go back to college.

Then I asked him this question, "What part of grad school has you most worried?"

"Writing," he said. "Grad school requires a lot of writing and I've never been a good writer." Now we had not only identified the real fear, but we had it in a corner. It wasn't grad school that was scary, it was the assumption that his success depended on his being a good writer. Improving his writing skills looked a lot smaller than failing grad school. Fear wanted him to think that because he wasn't naturally gifted at writing, he couldn't become a skilled writer, and even bigger still, couldn't get his advanced degree.

The fourth thing I do to defeat fear is I attack it.

In my friend's case, I was able to share tips and resources that would help him be a strong writer while going to school. Ideas like, working with peer groups to edit his papers; using his time management skills to get early drafts of his papers to his professors for review and feedback before turning in the final versions; and taking advantage of online grammar and writing tools such as Grammarly and Ginger. These were concrete actions he could see himself taking and set a goal to enroll in college the next day.

What are you afraid of? See if you can identify what's really keeping you from your Ideal life. Start by identifying what you really want. Then decide what you're afraid of that's holding you back. Then address the fear(s). Say, "I see you fear of   , and I'm not going to let you stop me from living my ideals." Then, fearlessly, go after the smaller issues and clear a path to your goal.

Plan of attack

What is something that you have bean fearful or apprehensive of? _____

Now let's break it down...

What part of this really concerns me? _____
_____

Why does this concern me? _____
_____

What strategies or resources can I utilize to address that concern? _____
_____

Chapter 5

Our Past Experiences Live Among Us

Why was I thinking about the time I was certain all the students in my grade school would laugh at me, 20 years after that incident happened? The same reason that a lot of people worry about setbacks, heartbreaks, mistakes, painful situations, and bad choices, sometimes days, weeks, months, and even years later.

Ghosts.

Research shows that often our brain doesn't record situations and experiences accurately. We tend to remember the "big stuff" first and make some assumptions about the rest of what happened. We also embellish the further away we get from the actual incident.

For instance, if you were reprimanded harshly by a parent when you were younger, when describing the incident, your brain will first remember "mom yelled at me." And you might remember being in trouble because you were very bad, because that's what you would expect from a scolding.

Similarly, you might recall losing your first job and exaggerate that your boss was a total jerk or that you were woefully unqualified for the job, when neither of those may be true.

Our brain makes up a story to make sense of something we don't actually understand. I call these "ghost stories."

Later, down the road, when someone admonishes us about our work, our driving, or how we treat them as a friend or partner, we think we're bad. Having the experience of being yelled at changed us in some way. Specifically, it changed our brain to allow us to re-visualize a scolding—that is, to reexperience the scolding, at least to some extent. Memory

Lane can also be paved with emotions, which can become the strongest part of the recollection.

The ghosts of our past experiences keep us trapped.

Imagine that you are planning to travel, and you need to book a hotel. You go online to find a nice place at a good rate. You find the perfect place with a surprisingly good rate, in fact, you can't believe it. You read the reviews. People say that it's a quiet place; they felt like they had the place to themselves.

One review calls it "the best kept secret." But further searching pulls up a press release from years past about an incident where several people mysteriously drowned in the hotel pool.

Chances are you're not booking that hotel, no matter how ideal it looks online. Or, if you do, while you might check out the pool, it's not likely you'll dive in. The hotel now has ghosts.

In the same way, ghost stories of the past can keep us from living our Ideal life.

Very real experiences—being scolded, fired, or dumped by a lover, can, if we're not careful, dictate what we do in the future. A memory, especially one with strong negative emotions attached to it, can keep us from believing that good things—Ideals, are even possible.

Ghosts are going to keep Jennifer from getting the job she wants.

Jennifer took the time to identify the things she wanted in her dream job. She went online and found jobs that matched her criteria and applied to as many of them as she could. She didn't hear back on some positions. For others, she interviewed but didn't move on to the final round of interviews and job offer. She came to believe that it was going to be impossible to get her dream job. She remembered not getting into her first choice for college. She also remembered her girlfriend's feedback to be more concise in her responses to interview questions. Jennifer went back to her criteria and downgraded her dream job.

Instead of a senior-level position, Jennifer started applying to manager and specialist roles.

I don't blame her. We all have ghost stories of not being good enough, a memory of something that didn't work out, or when you weren't the chosen one. It hurts. To protect ourselves, we pick lesser goals or make our dreams smaller.

We settle for what we can get, and we call it "good" because at least it's something.

But it becomes difficult to live a life full of passion when you are caught settling.

A friend of mine's mother-in-law suddenly developed vertigo while she was staying with him and his wife. One night, while walking to the bedroom, she said the room began to spin violently, and as a result, she took a nasty fall. They took her to Urgent Care where she was diagnosed with vertigo. She hadn't broken anything when she fell, but she would have bruises for several weeks. The doctor prescribed bed rest and a steroid to reduce inner ear inflammation.

While his mother-in-law got redressed, the doctor pulled my friend and his wife aside and had another conversation in the hall. He told them that her body would heal but that her confidence would take much longer to recover. He was right, it took several years for his mother-in-law to walk with confidence and overcome a fear of being alone for fear that she would fall again.

Ghost stories are tough to overcome because they are based on real past experiences--maybe not entirely accurate memories of what happened, but what's certain is that you lived through something that the brain recalls pretty forcefully.

But ghost stories are just fears in a detailed narrative format.

Identify your fears, isolate them, and attack them. Do it today. Create a new narrative. Do that, and you will remove one of the biggest barriers that holds us back from living our Ideal life.

What Ghost Stories do I need to rewrite?

_____

_____

_____

_____

Chapter 6

Our Beliefs and How We See Ourselves Are Sometimes Our Biggest Obstacles

"He who believes is strong; he who doubts is weak. Strong convictions precede great actions"

J.F. Clarke's quote emphasizes how much beliefs have to do with success or failure. I define beliefs as assumptions and convictions we hold to be true based on past experiences. Our potential, that is, what we can become or do as well as what we deserve in life, are all rooted in our beliefs.

"What is the most powerful determinant of potential?" is one of my favorite questions to ask an audience. I learned this question from The Pacific Institute. I give the audience the options of *Habits, Attitudes, Beliefs*, and *Expectations*. I let them talk to the person next to them or at their table and there's always a lively discussion. Then I make them vote.

Most often, people raise their hand for *Attitude*, with *Beliefs* and *Habits* tied for second and *Expectations* bringing up the rear.

People are usually surprised to learn that of the four, research shows *Beliefs* to be the most important, hands down (keep in mind that all four are extremely powerful and all four need to be addressed for true sustainable change).

Beliefs help shape habits. Most of our habits, from morning routines to exercise regimens, are daily activities we do without too much thought, in the *belief* that they are good for us. Unfortunately, we can also mistakenly believe bad habits are good for us.

"I play better when I'm high."

That's what a promising Division 1 college football running back told me when I met with him in his dorm room. I'd been called in to talk to him after he'd tested positive a second time for marijuana and as a result was being released from the team and losing his scholarship. When I met him, he was really angry and confused.

After talking with him, I realized he didn't just have a behavior or a drug problem, he had a belief problem. Since he could point to high school games, along with his college career, when he'd played well while he was stoned, no matter what behavior modification program the Athletic Department put him through, this young man would still believe that it served him to smoke weed. The coaches of this promising football player approached me because of the young man's habit, but his habit was a result of an erroneous belief.

I told him I wasn't convinced he had his facts right and asked him to consider some additional facts—including what results he could get if he were drug-free, and to also bear the responsibility for having made choices that now impacted his ability to continue to be on the team. He was bringing forward past bad habits expecting the same results, and it had caught up with him. We agreed there were good reasons for him to let go of his belief, and in so doing, he was also able to let go of his anger.

I think people always vote for Attitudes as the #1 determinate of potential because attitudes are often reflected in people's behavior; we think we can see a person's attitude by the way they are acting, whereas we can't see what a person believes.

When I first approached the football player, right away I could see his attitude, but his attitude was an emotional response to his belief.

A positive attitude is an optimistic belief that something good is going to happen. A negative attitude expects failure or bad results. When we believe something is good for us, we have a positive attitude toward it;

if we believe something is going to be boring or a waste of time, we have a negative attitude toward it. Beliefs shape attitudes. Attitudes are an emotional response to a belief that are then reflected in a person's behavior.

Ever sworn off a certain food that you've actually never even tasted? I have a friend who doesn't like peas. What is it about peas that causes such a negative attitude? It's her belief that they are going to taste like little musty, soggy cardboard bombs. Maybe it's the smell. It might also be that she read somewhere that peas are used as a prop to simulate vomit in movies. That makes them undeniably nasty. She wouldn't dare eat them. She also wouldn't wish them on anyone she likes and to this day, there has never been a pea served at her dinner table. Her kids actually think she's allergic to peas, and she's good with that.

The point is, attitudes are very powerful, and they are a response to what we believe.

Very few people vote for *Expectations,* but that doesn't mean we should underestimate their power. Expectations are a strong belief that something is going to happen in the future, and since we often get what we expect, expectations can help us reach our potential.

Professor of Social Psychology Scientist Robert Rosenthal and School Principal Lenore Jacobson conducted an experiment at an elementary school to study the effect of teachers' expectations on students' results. Rosenthal gave an IQ test to the students, and then told the teachers that a random group—not based on the test results, should outperform others. Their work showed that if teachers believed certain students were smarter, then the child's performance would improve. The study supports the phenomenon that people perform better when greater expectations are put on them.

When we believe strongly in someone or something we give it more attention, which can impact actual results, even if the belief is based on a fallacy.

I began to develop a beard when I was 13-years-old. Scientific research can tell you that we associate distinctive facial hair with maturity, power and status, so it was pretty cool to be one of the few guys in middle school with stubble. Before I even had enough to rock a goatee, people were noticing. By high school, I had a beard and it was part of my identity. I looked like a man—a baby-face with facial hair, but a man, nonetheless.

One of my friends asked me how he could grow a beard.

"Peanut butter," I said jokingly, referring to something I'd heard that if you put peanut butter on your face in the places that you wanted the hair to grow, it would sprout like a Chia Pet.

Months later, a group of us were at his house, hanging out and watching TV before heading to a party. At some point, my friend left the room. A few minutes later, he reappeared and sat down on the couch.

We all burst out laughing.

He'd spread peanut butter on his face in the shape of a beard.

We couldn't control our laughter, and my friend just sat there, unphased. He let us know that he'd been doing this for weeks. And he thought it was working; he believed he was growing more facial hair. Then he asked me how much longer it would take before he could expect a beard like mine.

I didn't want to but I had to tell him I'd been joking about the peanut butter. I felt bad, especially if having a beard on his face meant so much to him. He still reminds me about the peanut butter to this very day.

The best way to reach your potential is to believe you can, which is why believing you can achieve something is so powerful.

Where do beliefs come from? Beliefs are formed by:

- Our experiences,
- What we tell ourselves is true, and

- What other people tell us is true

The most powerful of those is what we tell ourselves, our own self-talk, because that voice is in our head every day. That's the voice that tells us we can do something great. It's also the voice that says, "This isn't going to work."

New research claims that each of us has between 50,000- 70,000 thoughts per day. Additional research states that for most people, most of those thoughts are negative.

If your brain is churning out that much material, the question is, are your thoughts positive or negative? It's an important question. As my mentor Lou Tice used to say, "Those thoughts don't just vanish into thin air; they build upon each other to form beliefs."

This is key. Our self-talk impacts our self-image, which feeds our sense of self-worth, and even determines how big we will allow ourselves to dream.

I often do an exercise where I will ask individuals or teams to "imagine…"and then describe the biggest dream they came up with. More than likely, at some point in the process, their self-talk kicked in and impacted the dream. If I ask them if they think their dream is possible, they start to doubt themselves and back away from it.

"It might be a little too big for me." "I think it's possible, unless…" "Maybe, except that…"

Negative thoughts stifle our ability to think in Ideals. They cause us to reduce the size of our goals to something we believe is possible for us to accomplish. The fault in that is that over time, we settle for less than what's Ideal. And that's when we feel unfulfilled.

Once, through a good friend who was an ambassador, I had the opportunity to meet the President of a country in Africa. I was excited. And honored. Until my negative self-talk got loud, at which point my brain invited doubt (based on fear) to join the pity party too.

What did I have to offer the President of an entire country? It was crazy of me to think I was the right person for the job. I was 28-years-old. I'd been in my consulting career for less than a year. I'd only been overseas once in my life. Why was I taking on such a big project--even though it was in line with my Ideals?

My thinking was straightforward: If I tried and failed, I'd look a fool. The surest way to not look a fool then, was to not try.

My belief was that I needed more experience, more international clients, more time—I just needed to be overall "more" before I was qualified to take on a project of this magnitude.

What's funny is that the President and members of his Cabinet believed in me more than I did.

Here's the thing about beliefs: sometimes they're created in such a subtle way. We don't just wake up one day and say, "I'm worthy!" Instead, we get there over time. The belief that we can do something— serve a client, be a good parent, reach our potential, live our Ideal life, is a result of years of experiences, self-talk and input from others. If that voice or input is positive, it can give us wings; if it's negative it can bury us.

Another thing to understand about beliefs is that they trump behavior every time.

I know, I know, there are lists and lists about the behaviors that will help you achieve your goals. Those are great. What's missing is the list of beliefs you need to achieve your goals, and how to adjust your beliefs if they're not helping.

Behavior alone isn't enough to achieve your goals because behavior isn't sustainable unless you know why you're doing something.

You exercise because you believe it makes you feel healthy and live well. You volunteer because you believe it improves your community. You set a goal to write for one hour every day because you believe it will make you a better writer and help you write a novel someday.

We focus on the activity because it's easier to see.

I'm here to tell you that every behavior is a result of a belief. When we change our beliefs about ourselves, our world, our lives, our communities, our families, we begin to act and respond differently. That can either put us closer to our goal, or farther away.

Darla was in an abusive relationship. Before getting into her situation, Darla had always been outgoing, smart, witty, and attractive. She'd enrolled in college to pursue her dream career.

After the first year in school, friends noticed a change in Darla. She spent less time with family and friends. She was evasive and didn't seem like herself. She stopped going to school. She told her mother she was in a new relationship. The next time her family saw her, Darla had bruises on her face.

Her family decided to intervene. They begged her to leave the relationship. Darla didn't seem to hear them. Finally, a family member stood up and said that if Darla didn't leave her boyfriend today, she was an absolute fool. Darla stood up and walked out.

I asked to meet with the family. I shared with them research that suggested that rather than give ultimatums or place shame, supporting Darla and encouraging her to make the right decision might help. I asked that anytime anyone saw or spoke to Darla, they validate her intelligence, speak to how talented she would be in her dream career, and reinforce what a wonderful person she was inside and out.

What's the saying about trust...it's built in drops and lost in buckets? The same can be true about believing in ourselves. It takes time to build it. And when we lose it, it can take time to get it back. In Darla's case, since she kept her distance from the family, things didn't get better right away.

Several months later, Darla's mom texted me. She asked me to come to her house quickly and said that Darla was there. I hoped everything was OK but expected something worse.

When I got to the door, Darla greeted me. She was radiant. She'd left the relationship.

One morning, she said, she woke up and told herself, "You deserve better."

Over time, her abuser had convinced her that she wasn't talented, beautiful or worthy of true love. Instead, he pointed out every flaw. She believed it, and once she did, she was willing to accept the abuse. In the beginning, the abuse wasn't physical, it was verbal, emotional and mental abuse. But once she believed she wasn't much of anything, it was easy for her abuser to prey on her physically as well.

Beliefs really are important because when we change our beliefs about ourselves, we begin to act and respond differently.

Darla reunited with her belief in herself. I want to underscore what a big achievement this was for Darla, or anyone in an abusive situation. Will she live her Ideal life? I hope so. For now, she's choosing to believe that she can.

What do you believe about yourself? Are your beliefs helping you achieve your goals or are they holding you back?

Spend a few minutes thinking about your dreams and whether you are pursuing them or have given up. Are you living your Ideal life? Remember, you only have one, so why not make it Ideal?

A Brief Self Assessment

How much do you agree with the following statements?

I can create my Ideal life:
❑ True ❑ Somewhat True ❑ Not at all True

I am resourceful:
❑ True ❑ Somewhat True ❑ Not at all True

I am good at finding solutions to my problems:
❑ True ❑ Somewhat True ❑ Not at all True

I have what it takes to be successful:
❑ True ❑ Somewhat True ❑ Not at all True

I deserve to be happy and fulfilled:
❑ True ❑ Somewhat True ❑ Not at all True

I have unbelievable potential:
❑ True ❑ Somewhat True ❑ Not at all True

I am confident:
❑ True ❑ Somewhat True ❑ Not at all True

I deserve the respect of my peers:
❑ True ❑ Somewhat True ❑ Not at all True

I am smart and capable:
❑ True ❑ Somewhat True ❑ Not at all True

I am good at accomplishing hard things:
❑ True ❑ Somewhat True ❑ Not at all True

Chapter 7

Are We Conditioned to Fail?

There's another barrier that stops us from thinking in terms of what's Ideal. It's conditioning.

When I say "conditioning" what do you think of? Maybe you think of physical conditioning and see an image of exercising or cardio-training equipment. Or maybe you think of a piece of dry wood or leather and the process you go through to treat it. You've got the right idea. Let's agree that conditioning is a repetitive process we go through to achieve a desired result.

The question is then, is your conditioning helping you achieve your Ideal life? Or is it keeping you from it?

There is no question that we are being conditioned for life. Every TV show, every ad, every tweet we see is conditioning us to think a certain way, behave a certain way, and purchase a certain item. We've been conditioned which restroom to use, what type of foods to eat, to look both ways before crossing the street, the list goes on and on.

Our dog, Mufassa, has me conditioned to walk him. Every time I come in my front door, he immediately gets his leash and brings it right to my hand. He'll stand there until I grab the leash and take him outside. The point is, people (fur people included) and experiences are conditioning us all the time. All this conditioning is intended to keep us safe, healthy, happy, and in line with social norms. In this way, conditioning is a good thing.

Unless it's bad.

If our conditioning is negative, all our beliefs about ourselves and the world become pessimistic. If our daily experiences and the people we have in our life, are gloomy, invalidating or unenthusiastic, then we can be conditioned for depression, anxiety and a sense of helplessness.

You can see then, why taking a close look at our conditioning is important. Ask yourself:

What have I been conditioned to believe about myself? When did I first start believing that?

Who taught me to believe that?

My parents conditioned me to believe that hard work pays off. They also conditioned me to believe that I could achieve any dream that I set my mind to. I was blessed in this regard; I was conditioned to believe in my potential. I was also conditioned to believe that all people are created equal and that all people deserve dignity and respect.

Other people may have been conditioned differently. If they were conditioned to play it safe and avoid risk, when they try to define their Ideals, it understandably makes them anxious. Their conditioning kicks in and all they can see is the danger. As a result, they downsize their Ideal.

Sometimes "good" conditioning can get in our way too. Because I believe that success comes from hard work, I'm conditioned to work hard. I think that my goals have to be difficult and I'm skeptical of anything that seems too easy. I'll even take a simple goal and challenge myself to make it bigger. Otherwise, I feel as though I'm not working hard enough. But it doesn't do me, or those around me, any good if I crawl across the finish line. So, I frequently check in with myself to make sure I'm doing the right work, not just the hard work. What does that look like? I'll ask myself, "Am I enjoying what I'm doing?" "Can I make this easier?"

Beware too, of the belief that you have to do it yourself--"it" being just about anything you want to accomplish, whether it's to start a new job, lose weight, or write your first novel. What's true is that while you are responsible for your life, it's nearly impossible to accomplish anything on our own.

Reaching your Ideal is going to mean relying on people and being conditioned to distrust or be anxious may keep you from your Ideal.

When I think about conditioning and the impact it has on our lives, I think about the weary traveler who stumbled into a village after walking all day in the sun. The local people rushed to his aid and led him to the drinking hole. They gave him water to resuscitate him.

As the traveler recovered, he was overcome with emotion and thanked the villagers. He explained it had been so hot and he had traveled so far without water that he thought he would never drink again.

When he finished, one of the villagers asked him why he was carrying such a large sack of earth on his head in such hot weather, making his journey more difficult.

Another villager asked the traveler why he was dragging such heavy cement blocks behind him.

The traveler looked at the sack of earth and the cement blocks and he explained that he didn't know, and furthermore, he couldn't remember where he'd picked them up or how long he'd been carrying them.

In a similar way, while we're not carrying sacks of earth and cement blocks, I think it's fair to say that we all are burdened by things we have picked up on our journey. We may not remember when we started carrying it, but it's weighing on us all the same.

The good news is that we're not stuck carrying the negativity we may have been conditioned by.

We can set negativity down and continue our journey without it.

How do we do that? First, we need to know that we're carrying it.

When you think in terms of your Ideals, pay attention to the thoughts and feelings that come up. What's your self-talk like at that moment?

Are you saying, "I can't do this"? or "That will never happen"? That's limiting negative conditioning that's pretending to protect your goals when it's really killing them.

In the 2010 movie, Inception, the main character Dom Cobb, played by Leonardo DiCaprio, invades the dreams of others to steal their secrets. To redeem himself, he must plant ideas in another person's mind.

"An idea is like a virus," Cobb says in the movie. "Resilient. Highly contagious. And even the smallest seed of an idea can grow. It can grow to define or destroy you."

He's right.

Acting on ideas/thoughts is the most powerful force we have to determine our lives or change our future.

If your thoughts are liberating, uplifting beliefs, and your conditioning supports them, then you have the power to realize your Ideal. If your conditioning is preventing you from thinking in Ideals, then stop. Do this instead:

- Recognize negative self-talk for what it is: unhealthy conditioning that is holding you back from living your Ideal life.
- Identify the beliefs that are behind your negative self- talk.
- Define what your Ideal life would be (Tip: If you don't know what you want, at least move away from what you don't want).
- Condition yourself to be positive. Work on it every day. The more often you speak in the affirmative, the more easily your brain will make it a habit.
- Choose to change today.

What negative thoughts am I willing to put down today?

_____

_____

_____

_____

_____

Chapter 8

Getting Stuck on How

I didn't really know how to launch my consulting business. I didn't know how to get clients. I hadn't put together my "value statement" that would convince people that, at 27- years-old, I could lead their companies to unprecedented success.

I used to pace the house, thinking about how I could build my business. I was motivated by the fact that I had a mortgage and a wife. I was determined and certainly willing to do the hard work.

One time, since I was up and pacing any way, I decided to take the dog for a walk at 3 a.m. The whole time, I was thinking about how I was going to make my business work.

When I got home, I went into my office and started to write down my Ideals.

That's not possible, my self-talk told me. Not in a million years. How will you ever make that work?

I made a deal with myself. I promised myself that if I wrote for one hour, then I could go to bed--but the writing had to focus on what, and not how.

I started to imagine the ideal clients I wanted to work with, and because I wasn't worried about how, I listed them all: corporations, non-profit organizations, educators, athletes, and faith-based groups.

Next, I imagined the impact I wanted to have on these groups. Ideally, we would partner together and with their investment in me, deliver the results they expected.

How are you going to do that, my brain asked? I reminded myself that I was only imagining about what I wanted to do, not how I was going to do it, and I kept writing.

I wrote down the idea that my family could travel with me. Ideally, I wouldn't have to sacrifice time with my family to grow my consulting business.

I wrote down the salary I wanted, the people I wanted to hire and the culture I wanted to create. At the end of the hour, I had an Ideal picture of my business, but still no idea how to make it happen.

Sleep on it, my brain said. And I went to bed just as I promised.

When I picked it up the next morning, my brain was still giving me negative answers when I asked the question, "How..." All my responses were coming from a place of fear, which was causing anxiety and stress. Then I remembered the saying, "If you don't like the answers, then change the questions."

Instead of asking how, I asked myself what and why.

- What was I trying to accomplish?
- Why was that important to me?

By the time I'd answered those two questions, I was sold. I knew I could build my Ideal business.

Asking *what* and *why* first, puts *how* in its place. *How* comes later. *How* sits in the wings until *what* and *why* have focused your brain and then you can take on *how.* .

When we start with figuring out how we are going to do something, we tend to create long lists of tasks that suck the air and passion out of a project. Don't get me wrong, To Do lists are a helpful part of the strategic planning process. But they're also an opportunity for the brain to tell you why something can't be done. Each "to do" has its own "to do" and soon your list is really long, and your self-talk is telling you it can't be done, and you quit. Or your focus becomes crossing things off the list, and not about the Ideal end goal. You're stuck in the *how*.

We've been conditioned to think and problem solve. If you want to create an extraordinary Ideal life, we can't think like most people. Figuring out the *how* is important to any goal, but when it is done out of place and out of order it does more to stifle creativity than to help us achieve our Ideal outcome.

Research shows that our brain likes goal *getting*. When we set a goal and then accomplish it, our brain rewards itself with a hit of dopamine. The problem is the brain can't tell the difference between a small task on a To Do List and an Ideal goal. When you tick off a small task, dopamine in your brain spikes, and your brain will want you to repeat the behavior. The risk here is that you repeatedly make lists and never get around to actually pursuing what you truly want in life. By starting with the Ideal picture first, you'll create the intrinsic motivation and passion that is required to live a fulfilled life.

Laura was very process-driven, and it showed up in every aspect of her life. She created spread sheets and lists for everything. The year I met Laura, she was planning the family vacation. She had organized an amazing trip, with every detail accounted for. Except one.

How did she want her family to feel at the end of the vacation?

The first thing she should have done is simply ask the question, "What matters?" to every person in the family.

For example, her teenager might have wanted the opportunity to do activities with other teens. Her husband may have wanted a fishing excursion. She may have wanted time to read her book around the pool.

The goal is to make sure that everyone has an opportunity to enjoy their Ideal at some point in the vacation. Then Laura can book the best destination, hotel and activities to make that happen.

Processes are a company's To Do List. Processes that are supposed to help companies improve efficiency can get out of control too. In a study of U.S. and European companies, The Boston Consulting Group found that over the past 15 years, the amount of procedures and decision approvals has increased anywhere from 50 percent to 350 percent.

Managers are also spending more time writing reports and attending meetings.

I've even coached leaders who have allowed process to become their culture. And we wonder why employees are disengaged.

When you roll out a new process or an audacious goal at work, start by inspiring a shared vision, and provide your employees with a sense of meaning and purpose for what you are asking them to accomplish. Do that, and you'll help employees focus on the "why," not just the "how." You'll also communicate that you value people over process.

PHASE 3

REALIZING OUR IDEAL

OUTCOMES

Chapter 9

Focus on what you DO want

To realize your Ideal outcome, you need to focus on what you do want instead of what you don't want. This sounds simple but I can tell you that we have been conditioned to focus on the negative in our lives.

Remember the concept of teleology and how the mind receives no picture from the word "Don't." By focusing on what you don't want, you actually bring those things, or the essence of those things, into your life. My friend and consultant John McNeil calls this the "Eastman Kodak" principle, because the original photographic process produced a negative, which was then used to produce a picture.

If your team is mired in a situation or a project, try this exercise:

Have everyone in the room to write down what they want to have happen. Give them time to think and make their list.

When time is up, ask them to read their list. I'll wager that people listed more items that they DON'T want. They might have listed that they don't want silos across teams to continue. They don't want to add another meeting to their calendar, or they don't want employees to disregard the new policy.

The point is, people are drawn to images and word pictures and focusing on what you don't want will actually lead your brain in the wrong direction. It's actually more like no direction, because when you focus on what you don't want, you don't really move toward anything. You're not moving toward your Ideal, your focus and energy is wasted trying to make sure bad things don't happen, and you haven't yet defined what you DO want.

Focusing on what you do want is life changing. As I mentioned earlier, when you focus on what you do want, you will start to see opportunity all around you. It's also a great way to attract the Ideal outcome to you.

Try this:

Get a blank piece of paper. Draw a line down the center. At the top of the left-hand column, write Don't Want. Then, make your list.

Next, on the top of the right-hand column, write Do Want.

Finally, change all your "Don't Want" items into "Do Want" items.

Your paper should look like this:

EXAMPLE

Don't Want	Do Want
A long commute	→ To work locally within 20 minutes
To be micro-managed	→ Autonomy
To work graveyard shift	→ 1st, 2nd or swing shift
To work with large groups of people	→ Small teams or independent work

BLANK COPY

By focusing on what you do want, and using positive language, you will breathe life into your Ideal.

Chapter 10

Look Like/Feel Like Fixed

n Phase 2, you identified the things that have been holding you back. Now let's create Ideal replacement pictures.
Start by answering two questions:

- What does Ideal look like fixed?
- What does Ideal feel like fixed?

One summer I wanted to fix my backyard. The family was larger, our kids were older. The yard wasn't working for us anymore and as a result, we hardly ever used it. The problem was, I didn't really have a picture for what I wanted back there; I just knew I wasn't happy with what we had.

I took a piece of paper and wrote Look Like at the top. On the other side of the paper, I wrote Feel Like. Turning the paper back over, I started to list what the backyard would look like after I'd fixed it. Mind you I didn't have such details as the number of lawn chairs or the botanical names of the flowers we'd plant. What I wrote was, "a place for kids to play." "A place for adults to entertain." "A place where my wife and I can lay in the sun."

Then I flipped the paper over. Under the heading, Feel Like, I wrote, "It feels safe." "Relaxing." "Fun," and "Oasis."

Now I had my Ideal image.

And here's what we ended up with:

The yard is a series of informal spaces that melt into each other. There is a place for kids to run and play that includes a clubhouse, slide, swings, and climbing wall. There's also a space that has a stone patio and a fire pit, where friends and family sit, make smores and laugh. The two spaces are bound together by a lawn framed by layered plantings that makes a nice place to sit in the sun, practice cartwheels or place the bouncy house.

Your turn. Identify one area of your life that seems like a mess. It can be a small thing like a cluttered playroom or a big thing like a personal relationship that's not working out. Now sit down and write down what it will look like and feel like when you fix the current situation and have your Ideal space or relationship.

Backyard
Looks like

A place for kids to play

A place for adults to hang out

Beautiful

A place for my wife and I to lay out in the sun

Feels like

Fun

Oasis

Relaxing

Safe

Chapter 11

What's Ideal?

Leadership coaches will tell you that if you want to get commitment and achieve what you set out to do, you must model the behavior you expect of others. You have to set the example.

As you grow your practice of thinking in Ideals, it's helpful to have models who have demonstrated the actions I talked about throughout this book. Take the time to find models.

Notice that I said models, and not mentors.

Mentors are people who invest their time and effort to help you along your journey. They're incredibly valuable. I've mentioned several mentors in my own life, beginning with my parents. Mentors can also be models, and certainly my parents set the example through their daily actions that they were committed to each other and I certainly learned a lot of valuable lessons from them about relationships and parenting.

Models are people you observe and then consider what you could do differently to enhance your life.

Where do you find models?

They're everywhere. Observe people. They can be people at work, in your neighborhood, and at your place of worship. They don't have to be people that you know personally. They can be people you never meet your entire life. In fact, models don't even have to be people; they can be places and things (people create mood boards, which are a type of collage of images, text and samples, as models for their remodel or makeover, for example). Given all that, realize that there are endless models to help you develop your Ideal.

My faith is modeled after the saints in the bible as well as others who I've never met but are still living today.

Parts of my business and the culture we created at Potential Unleashed were modeled after successful businesses from all over the world; companies doing things that either I saw firsthand or read about and thought would be Ideal for us.

One for my business is a company out of Kansas City called LeaderFuel Center, led by Denise Mills, a good friend and mentor of mine. When I first met Denise, I fell in love with the way she ran her firm and how her team customized solutions for their clients. I wanted to build something similar, with my own flavor, in my corner of the world.

My leadership style is a combination of my beliefs and values as well as leaders I've worked for, including Raymond Yee and Matthew Schmoker. They are both great at building and empowering teams. They also build cultures of trust, innovation, and high performance.

I've modeled my parenting style after so many amazing parents I've met throughout my life, from my parents and in- laws, to parents of my children's friends--even successful business leaders who I admire for growing their company while also being present and fully engaged for their families.

When you find a model, focus on their behaviors and practices. Pay attention to how you feel when you are in their presence.

When you observe a person you admire, how did s/he/they talk? How did they engage with others? When you walk into someone's home that makes you feel warm and welcomed, pay attention to what it is about the space that made you feel that way. What are the colors, fabrics and light sources in the room?

Also try out the behaviors that you observe. Experiment. It's important to be authentic and not just repeat what you see. You don't want to go through life trying to live someone else's life; but you can take behavior from different models and figure out if it will be effective for you.

Once you've picked up a behavior or skill that you've admired, how do you assess whether it's effective for you? Ask yourself whether the behavior matches who you are. If you are speaking or acting in a way that isn't consistent with your values or your Ideal, stop.

Another good idea is to ask a friend or colleague for feedback.

An Ideal Blueprint

The items we've discussed throughout this book are intended to help you think in Ideals going forward. Let's see if we can put it together in a construct that you can keep in front of you to remind you to make the changes we've discussed here.

I want to introduce you to the final tool, The Ideal Life Balance Wheel. To use the Ideal Life Balance Wheel, start by writing down the different areas that make up your life. Write down things like Family, Community, Health, Career, Marriage, etc.

After you have identified the different areas, ask yourself, what would be Ideal for each area.

Next, ask:

- What does Ideal look like fixed?
- What does Ideal feel like fixed?

Take the time to express what you really want for each of these areas and why this would be Ideal for you.

Once you have completed The Ideal Life Balance Wheel, you'll find it easier to think through how to create the Ideal picture.

EXAMPLE

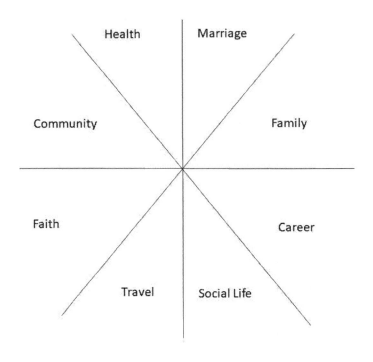

LIFE BALANCE WHEEL

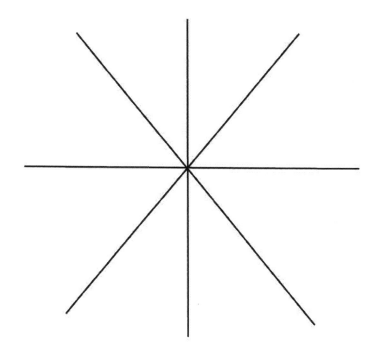

Additional Tips

Once you have decided what is I(deal) for you and your life, follow these next few steps.

1) **Get it out of your head**. Put your vision down on paper or in some kind of physical form. Draw a picture, make a 3D model, create a vision board. An important step in manifesting your Ideal is to get things out of your mind and into the world. Writing down your vision/goal is a great first step. If you are a visual person, pictures also work great!

2) **Put it up on a wall.** Once you have your vision down on paper, in a vision board, or some kind of 3D model, put it up on a wall. Put it somewhere you will see it every day. Choose a place in your home where you can guarantee you will engage with it every day multiple times a day. Choose a refrigerator, bathroom mirror, or another special place in your bedroom. There is a lot of power in being reminded about what you are moving toward every single time you grab a glass of water, brush your teeth or rise out of bed.

3) **Take small steps every day.** This is probably the most important tip, do something to move you toward your Ideal every single day. We often get stuck in trying to accomplish the miraculous. Many people believe that in order to achieve a goal or Ideal life that it requires some big act. I'm here to tell you that the magic is in the consistency. A great mentor once told me that if you

can just commit to doing 1 thing (no matter how large or small) toward your goals every single day, you will look up and be light years ahead of most people who rely on the large miraculous actions to accomplish their goals. I will go as far as to say that working toward your Ideal every single day is miraculous within itself. Stay focused and know that you have got this. What are you going to do today to move you closer to your Ideal?

Conclusion

I need to amend something I said earlier in the book.

I said I was a transformation consultant. I'm also a hope dealer. That's right, I(deal) Hope.

I travel the world inviting people to live their Ideal life. It's a service that people are demanding. Why? Because I think we know something is missing and we have a sense that we aren't living up to our full potential.

In my travels, I reach thousands of people, but that's not what I want. My Ideal is to help as many people as possible. Maybe you were at my presentation and wanted more information. Maybe you had a clarifying question and I couldn't answer it. Or maybe you're doing your own discovery and picked this book up along with other self-help manuals.

Either way, you've started, and I hope you accept my invitation to make the changes I know are possible.

I hope you see all the reasons we don't think in Ideals for what they are—excuses designed to hold us back.

I hope you break through the barriers that get in our way, and you stop thinking in terms of what you don't want and start using positive language. Repeat after me, "I want what's Ideal for me!"

I hope you use the Balance Wheel to clarify your Ideal life, including what Ideal looks like and how it makes you feel.

So deep and true is my desire for you to be successful, I am offering you support. You may reach me at www.idealthebook.com. I will make every effort to respond quickly and do everything I can to help you reach your potential.

I mentioned earlier that these are the tools and strategies that I have used to overcome obstacles and move toward my own Ideal pictures. I'm on a continuous journey in my life to become a better father, husband, son, brother, community member, mentor, servant, leader, and so much more.

Sometimes I completely miss the mark. Because I have an Ideal picture, I'm able to course correct and get back on track pretty quickly. It hasn't always been easy, but it has all been worth it. I believe in where I'm going and what I'm aiming for.

If you don't believe it for yourself at this moment, trust me-- YOU CAN HAVE YOUR IDEAL LIFE. Use the tools in this book, and reach out to me and my team if you need support. We believe in you.

I leave you with this: I hope you have an abundance of love, happiness, adventure, and good health in your life. Most of all, I wish you many small moments in life that become your most treasured memories. Memories are powerful. Powerful, inspiring and they give us the strength to pursue our Ideals.

THE
BEGINNING

About the Author

Jahmad Canley

Jahmad Canley has an endless dedication to empowerment and education for all people. He is internationally known as a top level culture transformation consultant, peak performance coach, author and masterful story teller. Jahmad focuses on helping people and organizations accomplish their goals and full their potential in their personal,  professional, and organizational lives. His passion for helping others unleash their potential has provided him the privilege of working with top organizations such as Microsoft, Amazon, Western Union, USA Swimming and many more.

Getting his start in Organizational Development and Change Management over 15 years ago, Jahmad has assisted numerous organizations and people accomplish and exceed their goals. Now as the President and CEO of Potential Unleashed Consulting, organizations around the world utilize his unique experiences and ability to transfer Cognitive Science and Culture Transformation processes to improve performance and remove barriers to success at the root cause.

Jahmad's diverse client database spans markets, industries, environments, and 5 continents. He continues to serve corporations, educational institutions, non-profit & faith based organizations, professional and amateur athletic teams, law enforcement and many more. His training and consulting services have resulted in higher productivity, retention, and a myriad of positive results for each partnering organization. Jahmad also works with organizations to begin or continue their work on creating diverse, inclusive, and equitable cultures and environments.

No matter the audience, Jahmad's ability to combine his energy and passion with a sense of humor and innate sincerity enables him to connect with a wide range of audiences and empower them to achieve the growth and change they earnestly desire. Whether it is a keynote, workshop, or panel discussion, Jahmad's dynamic style keeps audiences engaged and walking away enriched.

"I have learned that most people all over the world want the same thing...a better world for themselves, their families, and their communities. What keeps us trapped is often the lack of know-ledge or the lack of a process. I believe that to truly serve others, we must provide them with both a process and knowledge. The hour is late, the time is short, the task is great and we have a lot of work to do." - Jahmad Canley

In addition to his work, Jahmad is a dedicated family man and community member. In fact you'll often find his wife and children traveling alongside him in support at various events. Jah-mad is also the founder of the Tacoma Gents program. Tacoma Gents works with young men of color in the 3rd to 5th grades teaching L.I.F.E. (leadership, image/integrity, financial literacy, and etiquette) skills. The program is now in it's 5th year in partnership with Tacoma Public Schools.

NOTES

NOTES

NOTES

NOTES

Made in the USA
Middletown, DE
19 October 2022

13101929R00057